LYNN HOLLYN'S
TOWN & COUNTRY CAT

Dear Aunt Millie, Birthday 1990

I know this past birthday was a special one, and I feel a special need to let you know how special you are to me. I know this is late for a birthday gift, but let it remind you that I think of you on many days — always with warm thoughts and memories full of Love.

Enjoy — Love,

Marty xo

Prose and Patterns by Lynn Hollyn with Mary Mietzelfeld
Calligraphy by Hindy Taub with Lynn Hollyn

Lynn Hollyn's Town & Country Cat

Paintings by Robert Goldstrom

Workman Publishing, New York

Published simultaneously in Canada by Saunders of Toronto, Inc.

Library of Congress Cataloging in Publication Data

Hollyn, Lynn.

Lynn Hollyn's Town & Country Cat.

1. Cats. 2. Cats-Pictorial works. I. Goldstrom, Robert. II. Title. III. Title: Town & Country Cat.

SF445.5.H64 1982 759.13 82-40389 ISBN 0-89480-214-3

Workman Publishing Company, Inc.

1 West 39th Street New York, New York 10018

Manufactured in Hong Kong

First printing~ September 1982

10 9 8 7 6 5 4 3 2 1

To Michael
for whom words
cannot express my love,
and Justin
who grew with the book
day by day

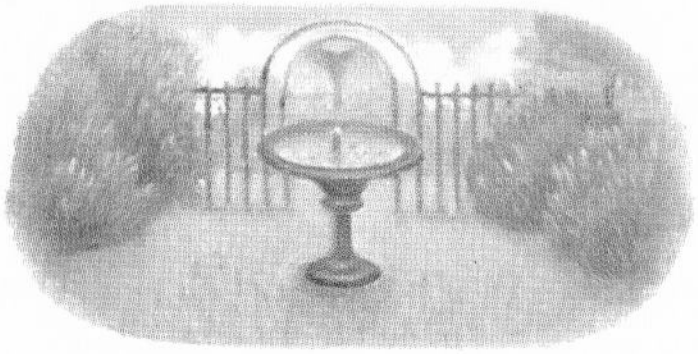

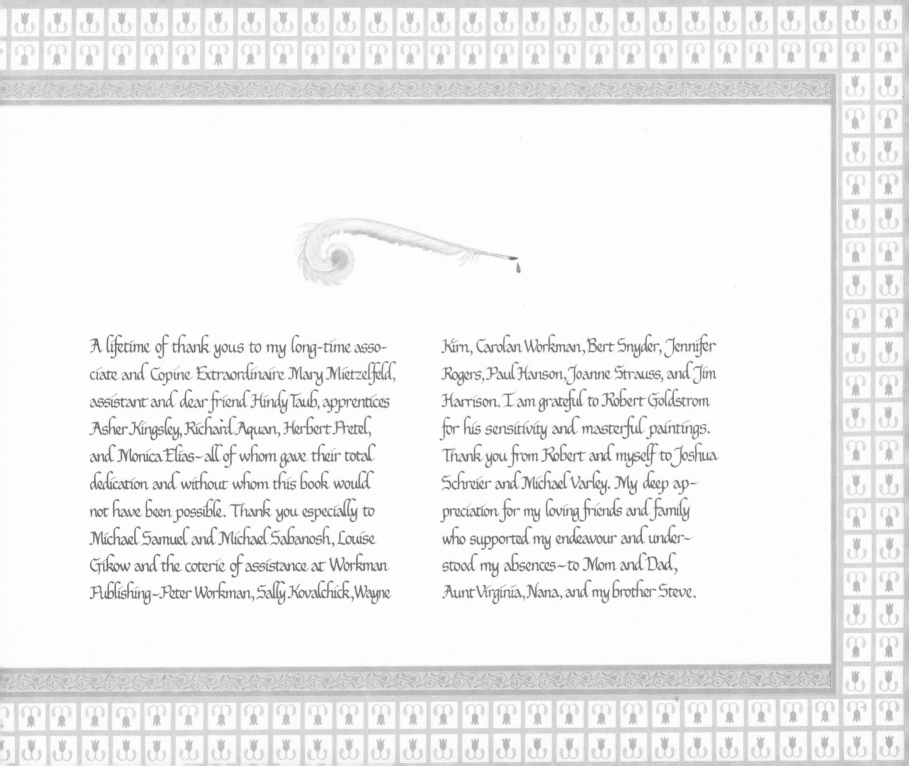

A lifetime of thank yous to my long-time associate and Copine Extraordinaire Mary Mietzelfeld, assistant and dear friend Hindy Taub, apprentices Asher Kingsley, Richard Aquan, Herbert Pretel, and Monica Elias—all of whom gave their total dedication and without whom this book would not have been possible. Thank you especially to Michael Samuel and Michael Sabanosh, Louise Gikow and the coterie of assistance at Workman Publishing—Peter Workman, Sally Kovalchick, Wayne Kirn, Carolan Workman, Bert Snyder, Jennifer Rogers, Paul Hanson, Joanne Strauss, and Jim Harrison. I am grateful to Robert Goldstrom for his sensitivity and masterful paintings. Thank you from Robert and myself to Joshua Schreier and Michael Varley. My deep appreciation for my loving friends and family who supported my endeavour and understood my absences—to Mom and Dad, Aunt Virginia, Nana, and my brother Steve.

In This Book

TOWN & COUNTRY ARTISTE

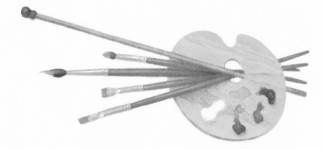

The elegant feline has graced our homes and our palaces through-out the ages; he has inspired literary sonnets and musical scores. The cat has been depicted in fiction and portrayed in the theatre and the ballet; he has ani-mated canvases and modelled for pho-tographers. From the concert hall to the writer's garret, Le Chat has been endowed with a mystique that fires the imagination. Writes Carl Van Vechten: "The poet... has seized the superiority of the cat and ex-alted it, perfumed it with exotic words, waved the incense of the grand phrase be-fore it, and anointed it with the holy oil of inspiration." Baudelaire captures this spirit:

"Because his voice is tenderly discreet;
   But let it be serene or vexed
Still always it is sonorous and profound,
   This is his charm and his secret."

Writers from Petrarch to Dickens have enriched our lives with memorable cat characters. We are indebted to Edward Lear for lovely Puss, who, as companion to an owl, went to sea in a "beautiful pea

green boat." Colette placed a Parisian feline in a scene of psychological conflict in which a husband is forced to choose between his wife and his pet. The wise cat of one of Kipling's "Just So Stories" cleverly bargains for his freedom with a cavewoman who proffers shelter: in exchange for capturing mice, he is permitted to wile away his days strolling the fields and countryside, revelling in the pleasures of solitude. And we cannot forget the Bard. Although most of Shakespeare's allusions to the cat are hardly complimentary, our most famous writer does somewhat begrudgingly accord the "harmless necessary cat" his irrepressible place in our lives.

Writers have often found cats to be in harmony with their own solitary natures. One of Theophile Gautier's cats was so attuned to his master that he nodded each time the writer lifted his pen to commence

a line of script. Swinburne describes the beguiling aloofness of the cat who both befriends and intrigues him—

"Stately, kindly, lordly friend
Condescend
Here to sit by me, and turn
Glorious eyes that smile and burn

Golden eyes, love's lustrous meed
On the golden page I read."
The twentieth-century Irish poet Louis MacNeice evokes a profound affection for cats in these lines:
"...this was a person
In a small way who had
touched our lives
With a whisk of delight, like a
snatch of a tune
From which one whole day derives."

The beautiful words of poet Neville
Braybrooke glorify his own cat, Foof:
"Half a life I have spent with cats,
or a cat, on my desk
I am not a much travelled man
Malta is the farthest south I have been
I remember the pumpkins growing wild
by the road's edge

Yet if I stare into the face of
my fifteen-year-old cat
I do not regret the lack of journeys
For when I look into his

contracting, dilating pupils
I travel in depth....

... at night I switch on the lamp
His eyes burn red in the glare
But when the morning breaks
The day fans these embers into
sapphire blue flames.
The afternoons remain more philosophical
Between tea and supper~
Across a desk strewn with papers~
Our eyes meet, blur and
reach the infinite."

The smallest feline
is a

Masterpiece

Artists have long honoured the luminous spectrum of the cat's persona, captivated by both his contours and symbolic potential. "Nothing is so difficult," observed Champfleury, "as to paint the cat's face. ...The lines are so delicate, the eyes so strange, the movements subject to such sudden impulses, that one should be feline oneself to attempt to portray such a subject." Despite the formidable challenge, artists have continuously struggled to capture the cat's essence. The attempt to immortalize the cat dawned with the rise of civilization. While the Egyptians created sleek and elegant bronze felines, the artists of the Far East reigned supreme in capturing the "domestic tiger with the grace of love, understanding of sympathy, and inescapable Oriental touch of mystery." Recall the fluid images of the floating world, playfully depicting the feline accompanying delicate, kimono-clad beauties, strolling with parasols in hand.

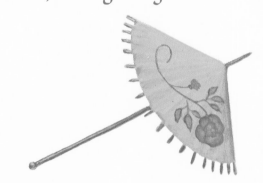

In medieval times, European artists emblazoned the feline on shields and

flags to represent the freedom and enlightenment they were seeking. Decorative cats were carved on religious edifices, and slyly slipped into the sacred masterpieces of the Italian Renaissance painters. A humble tabby is the centrepiece of Barocci's celebrated altar decoration, "La Madonna del Gatto." In Ghirlandaio's honoured fresco of "The Last Supper,"

the wise feline glowers at Judas. Leonardo da Vinci was intrigued by the evanescent nature of the cat - its chameleonlike expressions and ever-changing form. Later European painters, including Rembrandt and Velázquez, also picture the puss in their portraits and still lifes. Renoir captures the relationship of feline to human with languorous symmetry in his tableau of cat and boy, "Le Garçon au Chat."

The French illustrator Grandville is celebrated for his adeptness at capturing the unique personality of the cats he portrayed, costuming them and placing them in extravagant settings.

In Flemish paintings the cat is seen at home with the family, reclining by an iron stove or lapping up cream. The misanthropic, Hungarian-born Gottfried Mind was dubbed "The Raphael of Cats"; he required no other companionship and illustrated nothing but felines, imbuing them with vitality and infinite variety. In America, the cat has best been represented in the quaint and charming realm of folk art: the feline has been painted, embroidered, engraved, carved, cast, and appliquéd. The many images of the cat through the ages are testimony to his beauty as well as to his capacity to symbolize ideals for which we have no words.

The sounds of the feline have been likened to musical notes, and the harmonies of fugues and sonatas have been inspired by the sonorous cat. Composers

have created the instrumental equivalent of miaows, spits, and caterwauls. Tchaikovsky's "The Sleeping Beauty" has the famous portrayal of Puss in Boots and the White Cat dancing spiritedly to an orchestral imitation of feline sounds.

Ballet itself pays tribute to the litheness of cats with the complex dance step called the "pas de chat." In "Peter and the Wolf," Prokofiev's famous feline theme is played by a sly clarinet. And one of Scarlatti's compositions was inspired by his pet's dalliances upon the keyboard. Legend has it that the Swedish Nightingale, Jenny Lind, was discovered at the window singing fondly to her calico companion. Beginning in childhood, such nursery rhymes as "The Cat and the Fiddle" unite in our minds the harmony of music and cat.

Town & Country Courtship

Tomcat will court his chosen lady by circling about her till he senses that he's won her heart– at least for the moment. An enterprising Tom will have the wit to woo while the others brawl among themselves. As always, though, the female makes the final choice, languidly rubbing the ground around her chosen– sometimes even stroking his fur while kneading the earth with her paws. Cats, as anyone who has ever been awakened by one knows, are very vocal suitors, whose "sweet nothings" range from low-pitched cries to contented purrs of requited love.

"Beyond the fence she hesitates
And drops a paw, and tries the dust.
It is a clearing but she waits
No longer minute than she must."

Mark Van Doren

What are the signs of longing for love in your cat? As inscrutable as she is amorous, she will nonetheless not disguise her passion as desire overcomes

her. Even as a lovesick youth discloses new dimensions to his character, your cat will show you yet another facet of her prismatic personality. In every way she can, your female will tell you when her season approaches. She will cry and caterwaul, spraying her perfume about her realm. As if possessed, she will roll upon the floor and rub the furniture, needing to be touched as she needs food. Unlike the Queen, the Tom is always anxious to satisfy his unmistakable longings. But the lady in question may have more than one suitor, and as did knights of old, he must duel for her love ⸻.

"A dying ember...
in the abandoned cat, love
and the need of love."
J.W. Hackett

"Minette, your mistress you awake
By your drawn-out cry;
Would your ravenous hunger slake?
Is it a mouse you hear go by?
You would flee from my bed
To run to who knows where
Miaow-miaow; what's in Minette's head?
Miaow-miaow; a Tom goes there."
Pierre Jean de Béranger

"Kittens, than Eastern houris fairer seen,
Whose bright eyes glisten with
immortal green,

Shall smooth for tabby swains
their yielding fur,
And to their amorous mews,
assenting purr...
Fate, envy, curs, time, tide, and
traps defy,
And caterwaul to all eternity!"
George Huddesford

"In love you have a beautiful way
Never drawn by the scandalous cry
To the roof where gutter Toms lay
Despite your fires a lady you stay."
Mme. Deshoulières

The amorous cat is one of the most intense and haunted of all animals. The overwhelming strength of her yearning can often be distressing, perhaps because it reminds us of the frightening power of uncontrollable desire. For either Toms or Queens to be deprived in their season can be frustrating and cruel.

The choice of whether or not to alter is a hard one for most cat owners. As difficult as it can be to live with a cat who is not gelded, there is always the lingering question: will altering a cat physically alter it emotionally as well?

Will the tenor of its life be irrevocably transformed? If you opt not to alter your pet, you must be prepared to give rein to the eloquent desire of this most passionate and sensitive of creatures.

No Workman
Can Build a door
Proof Against a
Cat or a Lover

Everyone knows that cats will be lovers as often as they can, and with as many suitors as will offer themselves. But do cats "fall in love," that vaunted state that we tend to celebrate as a solely human province? Perhaps it is impossible for us to say with surety, but the French writer Théophile Gautier was convinced that the two white cats immortalized in his writings, Don Pierrot de Navarre and the lovely Seraphita, shared a life-long passion. Don Pierrot's sweetheart was as dazzlingly white as he was himself. Seraphita, for so

she was named in honour of a great Brazilian beauty, was gentle, dreamy, and contemplative. Don Pierrot, on the other hand, came from Cuba and possessed a hothouse temperament. The two were buried side by side in Gautier's garden, beneath a white rose tree that symbolized their union～.

"None the less, 'tis ours to suffer
That when cat love finds expression
In the night in sweetest numbers,
Men accord to us but scorning,
And they brand as 'caterwauling'
All our choicest compositions.
Yet, alas! 'tis ours to suffer
That these same contemptuous mortals
Call such sounds into existence
As I have been forced to hear.
Sounds like these are surely garlands
Bound of briars, straw, and thistles,

Where the stinging nettle flaunteth.
And in view of yonder damsel,
Grasping yon abhorrent trumpet,
Can a man with front unblushing,
Jeer when cats are making music?
Suffer, gallant heart within me,
Suffer! Times are surely coming
When the sapient human being
Will from us acquire the method
Of high feeling's right expression.
When the rude world, struggling...
Toward the climax of all culture,
Will appreciate 'caterwauling....'"
Hiddigeigei, the Tom Cat

The Young Man and His Cat

"A young man owned a cat with which he was wont to sport, and which he greatly loved. Day and night he prayed to Venus, that she show favour to him and to his cherished pet. The kindly goddess heard his prayer, and changed the cat into the most beautiful of maidens, whom the youth married that

very day. But alas! even on their wedding night, when the bride lay clasped in her husband's arms, she heard a mouse scamper across the

room, and leaped lightly from her bed to pursue it. Venus, angry at this profanation of wifehood, and perceiving that, however altered in form, a cat remains a cat at heart, changed her back into a beast, in order that soul and body might be in conformity———.

Aesop's Fables

Let us not forget to mention that aspect of feline love closest to your own heart: the courtship between you and your cat————. "Why, it is asked, should we humble ourselves to win the fluctuating affections of a cat... why indeed, save that some of us most desire that which is difficult to obtain; that some of us value most that which we fear to lose. When with delicate blandishments we have beguiled a cat from her reserve, when she responds, coyly at first and then with graceful aban-

don to our advances, when the soft fur brushes our cheek, when the gleaming eyes narrow sleepily, and the murmurous purr betrays the sweetness of her content, we feel like a lover who

has warily and with infinite precaution stolen from his capricious mistress the first tender token of possible surrender."

Agnes Repplier

Town & Country Temperament

The feline has aptly been celebrated for his independence, yet he will often adopt the expression and demeanour of his owner's personality. Your pet's temperament will reflect the seasons as well. In spring and summer, writes Repplier, cats will revel in the joyous garden life, enjoying repose and contemplation, venery and sport— "The odour of rose and jasmine, the tall trees on whose branches unsuspicious birds nested and sang, the miniature rocks circling the fountain, amid which she lay concealed like a Lilliputian tiger in its lair, all these wonders enraptured her sensitive soul."

As summer winds turn chill, your velvet-eared companion will prefer the luxury of the warming fireside and mesmerizing dance of the crackling flames.

Do cats think? If so, their thoughts are masked by their aloof facade, their equipoise. The English scientist

St. George Jackson Mivart quipped, "We cannot, without becoming cats, perfectly understand the cat mind." Folklore and fantasy have filled us with notion that our four-footed friends are endowed with memory and cunning, and experience emotion, passion, pleasure, and pain. On the other hand, the scientific community has generally scorned the idea of animal consciousness. Yet when we accidentally tread upon the tail of a furry feline, we know he has feelings. His plaintive miaow clearly indicates discomfort. How long is the feeling retained? How intense is the pain? He cannot tell us. But we believe that cats possess an acute consciousness. Scientists now question the degree

of feline intelligence, language, and emotion rather than their mere existence.

No two cats have the same personality. The sleepy-eyed, quiet pet of your tranquil abode appears strangely unrelated to those gregarious cats enmeshed in the furious activities of a newspaper office or police station, who thrive on their tumultuous surroundings and abandon themselves to the pleasures of

scurry and excitement. The feline mascot of a sailing ship swears unswerving allegiance to the hollow oak and the sea, flourishing in the changing scenery

of international ports of call. If your cat shares this wanderlust, he may like to join you on your outings. To cats so inclined, your Rolls-Royce is the closest thing to paradise. Sunning in the back window or curled up in front of the heater, he will be lulled to sleep by the automobile's deeper purr.

The cunning feline who slinks in the silver shadows of alleyways and basks by the golden flames of the hearth displays surprising acumen. Unlike people, cats never make the same mistake twice. One pair of ill-mannered young Persians in Austria had developed the habit of perusing the dinner table as the servants loaded it with food. As a maid brought a platter of cutlets one evening, the felines were startled by an explosion of gas in the kitchen. Although they resumed their strolls on the polished mahogany surface two weeks after their fright, the pair fled

the moment cutlets were once again served. Curiosity, a hallmark of intelligence, is a trait shared by all felines. It overwhelms them whenever a box lid is lifted, spurs them to jump as a breeze ruffles the blinds, and demands their investigation of footsteps upon the stairs. Wrote the masterful Carl Van Vechten: "To my mind there is no more doubt that animals think, after their fashion, than there is that men as a rule do not think at all."

Te salue en toi calme penseur
deux exquises vertus
scepticism et douceur

"It seems to understand us perfectly but care not a whit whether we understand it."

Théophile Gautier

"Philosopher and comrade, not for thee
The fond and foolish love which
binds the dog;
Only a quiet sympathy which sees
Through all my faults, and bears
with them awhile.

Be lenient still, and have some
faith in me,
Gentlest of sceptics, sleepiest of friends."

Jules Lemaître

A cat has "absolute emotional honesty:
human beings, for one reason or another, may hide their feelings,
but a cat does not."

Ernest Hemingway

She pretends "to sleep that she may
see more clearly."

Chateaubriand

Our image of the cat is of a solitary creature, but felines often form two-somes, strolling through the park or lolling on the verandah. In early evening or towards dawn, a congress

of cats enjoy one another's agreeable companionship in Roman piazzas and Parisian cafés. That venerable British periodical, "The Spectator," described the feline parliament that rules the capital each night ——.

"On summer mornings from four a.m. to five, London ceases to belong to the world of men, and is given over to birds and cats. At this real-ly bewitching hour, for the city then is beautiful, the cats may be seen, as at no other time, rerum domini,

masters of the town. It is not for nothing that the race has for generations maintained its independence, and asserted its right to roam. For at that hour all the

dogs are shut up, all the boys and grown people are asleep. The city is theirs. The demeanour of London cats at four a.m. is one of assured freedom. They stroll about the streets and gardens with a quiet

air of possession. They converse in the centre of highways. They walk with feline abandon and momentary magnificence over open squares. In the silver grey of a London dawn they are no longer domestic pets, they are gentlemen at large———."

Le Chat is seldom intrusive and rarely exuberant, but manifests at times a sweet and flattering desire to be with us. Ever respectful of our silence, he occasionally allows himself to be seduced into play. But although he can be the most gentle and loving of pets, Puss is above all a hunter and fighter who will retain his independence even in the most domestic of settings. As Méry observed, "God made the cat that man might have the pleasure of caressing the tiger." The country cat should be allowed to sport in field and garden, while the apartment-dweller must be compensated with a catnip mouse or peacock feather

to chase and pounce upon. However far he may stray from home, the domesticated cat instinctively seeks the familiar. Stories abound in which cats have embarked upon "incredible journeys" across continents to reunite with loving families who have moved to faraway towns.

Town & Country Kitten

"A kitten," declares Champfleury, "is the delight of a household. All day long a comedy is played by an incomparable actor." Kittens relish attention and applause, and a mischievous impudence and enchanting gaiety prompt them to their parts. Their frolicking captivates any audience, as their seeming innocence belies the coquetry behind their wondrous eyes. All the world, indeed, is a stage for these merry characters. They pirouette and pose with a performer's beguiling flair. "Everything that moves," noted F.A. Paradis de Moncrif, "serves to amuse them. They believe that all nature is occupied with their diversion." Secure in that feeling, kittens easily establish their dominion over their bemused admirers.

Even if you are bewitched by the captivating antics of that calico kitten in the pet shop window, you should always select a cat that is compatible with your family, home, and temperament. You can choose from short hair or long, male or female, and from as many breeds as there are colours. The elegant pedigreed Persian, the tailless Manx, and the neighbouring farmyard tabby

each have their charm. On kitty's arrival home, lift her gently from her carrier and lavish her with attention. Whatever her particulars, she will respond to milk and cream, love and warmth. A variety of toys, from a battered Ping-Pong ball to crumpled tissue paper, will help your kitten forget the brothers and sisters she has left behind. Make sure to provide a cozy sleeping spot to ease the separation from mother. Even if you ensconce your kitten in the most palatial of settings, tiny mews may still pierce your dreams that first traumatic night.

Food and play are the mainstays of a kitten's active life. Away from mother's tutelage, your kitten depends on you

to provide a nourishing, stimulating environment. Once weaned, kittens have insatiable appetites. Gratify their glut-

tony with high protein foods to build up their little bones and muscles.

"Kittens you are very little
And your kitten bones are brittle,
If you'd grow to Cat's respected,
See your play not be neglected."
Oliver Hereford

Kittens are eager explorers. Consumed with excitement, and trembling with the anticipation of discovery, they will chase a butterfly, foray into the dark recesses of your pantry, or scramble up your silken draperies. Even the youngest feline exibits an aristocratic love of finery. Why else would she nestle amid your satin sheets and ermine fur?

Maternal affection is the only sentiment in a cat's heart that can compete with her devotion to her master. Love for her kittens will always triumph. Nothing exceeds the courage and devotion of Mother Puss when danger threatens her young. St. George Mivart tells of a cat who plunged into a swiftly cascading brook to rescue her drowning kittens. During the London fire of 1884, a new mother rescued three of her offspring and perished in a brave attempt to save the fourth. The father assumes a protective role as well. Replier writes of an English Tom who "...took the athletic training of his children entirely upon his own capable shoulders, teaching them assiduously to climb trees, to scale walls, and to

spring upon birds." While living in Paris with his wife, Hemingway entrusted his baby son to the "sensible, affectionate, yellow-eyed cat called F. Puss who sat erect, like a nanny, keeping guard."

a little lion
small and dainty sweet

with sea-grey eyes
and softly stepping feet

It is important to show your affection for your cat, who flaunts her independence yet craves tenderness. Enjoy her responses. She may stroke your face with her nose, arch her back, thrust

her head against your knee, or simply purr. While she needs your endearments, she must trust you absolutely for her to revel, or even show an interest, in your caresses. Affection fosters confidence. A cat who has not acquired trust and

assurance during kittenhood can mature into an insecure, timorous, or unresponsive adult cat. Like an infant, a kitten must be nurtured with love. Kittens who are frequently handled respond earlier to outside stimuli and are more sociable, curious, and resilient.

"The cat's energy is subdued into an exquisite moderation. Other animals employ roughly what strength they... possess, without reference to the smallness of the occasion; but the cat uses only the necessary force. One day I watched a kitten playing with a daffodil. She sat on her hind legs and patted the flower with her paws, first with right paw, then with the left, making the light yellow bell sway from side to side, yet not injuring a petal or stamen. She took delight, evidently, in the very delicacy of the exercise. This proportioning of force to need is evidence of refinement in manners and art."

Philip Gilbert Hamerton

"But the kitten, how she starts,
Crouches, stretches, paws and darts!
First at one, and then the fellow,
Just as light and just as yellow,
There are many now, now one,
Now they stop, and there are none."

William Wordsworth

"A female cat is kept young in spirit and supple in body by the restless vivacity of her kittens. She plays with her little ones, fondles them, pursues them if they roam too far, and corrects them sharply for all the faults to which feline infancy is heir. A kitten dislikes being washed quite as much as a child does, especially in the neighbourhood of its ears. It tries to escape the infliction, rolls away, paddles with its little paws, and behaves as naughtily as it knows how, until a smart slap brings it suddenly back to subjection.

Pussy has no confidence in moral suasion, but implicitly follows Solomon's somewhat neglected advice. I was once told a pleasant story of an English cat who had reared several large families, and who, dozing one day before the nursery fire, was disturbed and annoyed

by the whining of a fretful child. She bore it as long as she could, waiting for the nurse to interpose her authority; then, finding passive endurance had

outstripped the limits of her patience, she arose, crossed the room, jumped on the sofa, and twice with her strong soft paw, which had chastised many an erring kitten, deliberately boxed the little girl's ears,—after which she returned to her slumbers.... M. Dupont de Nemours gives a charming instance of grandmotherly care and devotion on the part of a cat whose young daughter was very ill after the birth of her first kittens. She had a little family of her own at the same time; but she gathered her grandchildren into her overflowing basket, nursed them, and watched over them attentively, until their parent was able to assume her maternal duties."

Agnes Repplier

Town & Country Care

To watch your cat primp and preen is an experience akin to observing a young girl before the mirror on the eve of her first date. Just as the would-be debutante will fret and fuss over every detail till all is perfect, so will the fastidious feline patiently toil until every whiskertip is in place and her fur is as lustrous and soft as velvet. The only difference in our two tableaux is the spirit that pervades them~ the one frantic with adolescent flutter, the other imbued with the meditative calm of a timeless rite. From what ancestral dandy comes the cat's legendary obsession with her appearance? It is just one more inexplicable facet of the "inscrutable, ineffable cat."

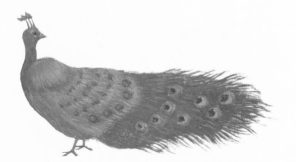

There is a practical characteristic of the cat dear to even the most romantic cat lover's heart, and that is her innate ability to care for herself. She will

acrobatically scrub the furthest tip of her tail with precision, poise, and a gymnast's agility. But however adeptly felines may manage their personal hygiene, few can resist the delightfully fur-tingling sensation of a daily grooming session. As you gently brush and massage your pet, you not only express your regard for her pleasure and well-being, you help take care of the excess fur that her tongue cannot remove. So soothing is her toilette that the cat in moments of embarrassment or frustration instinctively begins to wash herself, even as we may fidget with a strand of hair or adjust a collar when discomfitted by an unexpected situation.

Solitary though they may be, cats enjoy being pampered. Show your cat her inestimable place in your heart by setting aside a special place for her dining and slumber. Finding the perfect bed for puss is not always the simplest of affairs. The elegant, custom-made little basket you purchased may fail to entice her as it did you, so don't be crushed if she ever so delicately turns up her tiny nose in disdain. If she seems partial to napping beneath your covers, an old blanket folded in a cozy hatbox can approximate the

smell and feel of your own bed. Best of all, naturally, is if the two of you can happily occupy the same bed. But not everyone is partial to small, furry foot warmers. And however affectionate, the cold, wet kiss of a little nose at six in the morning cannot always be returned with unqualified enthusiasm!

Selecting china for your cat is a much simpler matter than resolving the delicate question of the boudoir. She will rarely be as fussy about her table setting, but whether it is purchased and decorated exclusively for her or is part of the family set, make it special. Your orderly pet finds it comforting to have everything in its proper place, and food will seem more pleasing to her palate in

her own sunflower-dappled saucer. Adult cats prefer to eat once or twice a day, but their repasts as well as their sleeping habits can be arranged around your own. If left to their own devices,

felines tend to nap and nibble throughout the day and night, scarcely differentiating between the two. But your pet will probably favour dining with you and slumbering when you are either at work or asleep, in order to luxuriate in the pleasure of your company⁓.

Puss on the hearth
with velvet paws
Sits wiping o'er his
whiskered jaws.

"Cultivate your garden said Goethe
and Voltaire,
Every other task is wasted
and dead-born;
Narrow all your efforts to
a given sphere,
Seek your heaven daily in
a bit of ground.
So my cat behaves. Like a veteran,
He brushes well his coat before
he sits to dine;
All his work is centered in
his own domain,
Just to keep his spotless fur

soft, and clean, and fine.
His tongue is sponge, and brush, and
towel, and curry comb,
Well he knows what work it
can be made to do,
Poor little wash-rag,
smaller than my thumb.
His nose touches his back,
touches his hind paws too,
Every patch of fur is raked, and
scraped, and smoothed;
What more has Goethe done,
what more could Voltaire do?"

Hippolyte Taine

Caring for your cat is like caring for any other warm and tender being. Most important are understanding and spontaneous, abundant affection. As you live together, the two of you will learn the practical considerations of day-to-day cohabitation, disovering as well all of friendship's happiest moments. Watch

over your pet. A healthy cat has clear and shining eyes, abundant energy, and a glistening soft mantle of fur. She will respond quickly and gracefully to each

new sensation or adopt the languid postures of the aristocrat. Your cat is a constant animal: any change in her habits should elicit your concern. If her fur has lost its lustre, or her eyes are clouded and her nose running, something is amiss. Cats are resilient, healthy, and full of a natural joie desprit. Common sense coupled with tender devotion will enable you and your feline to enjoy many years of happiness.

Town & Country Scholar

The paw prints of the ancient cat on desert sands have long been erased, but the feline has made an enduring impression in history. The cat, which seems to have descended from the African wildcat, first deigned to share the homes of the Egyptians some 5,500 years ago. The Egyptian families loved these furry creatures for the same companionship, beauty, and grace for which we cherish them today. Whether for their prowess in hunting rodents or their mystical qualities, they came to be revered as gods. In the ancient city of Bubastis, a temple was erected, dedicated to the cat goddess, Bastet, mistress of love and all matters feminine. The monumental sphinx embodies the union of human and feline—an icon surrounded by an aura of mystery—.

The feline has been an ever-changing presence throughout history. In Scandinavia, the cat was fabled as the protector of butter and cream; its quiet steps were associated with love's soft advances. The Arabian cat

was depicted as bold and daring, while the Greek Aesop moralized time and time again about the wisdom of cats. In the Middle Ages, reverence changed to fear, and cats were sacrificed as witches, but they soon regained their rightful place in the hearts of Europeans. Armies of rats had accompanied the Crusaders home, and seventy-five percent of Europe's population perished in the Bubonic plague that followed. The feline became the hero in the struggle against the rodent hordes and some historians credit the cat for the survival of European civilization. Thus by the end of the Renaissance, cats were once again comfortably settled by the cozy hearth.

Cardinal Richelieu, Louis XIII's advisor, insisted upon his kitten's attendance at court lest he become bored, and he remembered each one of his fourteen precious grimalkins in his will. Later, the feline's exquisite movements and refined nature allowed her to bask in the splendour of the Sun King's reign. The fashionable feline then became the beloved of the Beau Monde of the French bourgeoisie. In England, appreciation for Le Chat as an objet d'art ascended during the decorative epoch of Queen Victoria. The Victorians

sentimentalized and pampered their cats, linking them forever with the warmth of home:

"Around, in sympathetic mirth
Its tricks the kitten tries;
The cricket chirrups on the hearth,
The crackling fagot flies."
Oliver Goldsmith

The cat is the weathervane of Scotland and England and the timepiece of China. In Japan~"Land of the Rising Sun"~ the mooncakes which are baked for departed ancestors during the Festival of the Hungry Ghosts, are often associated with cats whose cyclical nature parallels the phases of the moon. The feline's iridescent orbs echo the lunar rhythms:

"Splendid circled eyes
that wax and wane for hours
green as green flame, blue grey like skies."
Agnes Repplier

Both the cat's nocturnal habits and her fertility support the association between the cat and moon. A tie also binds the grimalkin and the owl: both are luminous-eyed creatures of the night,

traditionally allied with wizards and witches, silhouetted harbingers of hallowed All Saints' Day~.

TO RESPECT
THE CAT
Is the   BEGINNING
                OF THE
                Aesthetic
                sense

Our bewhiskered friend has long been associated with a realm beyond our ken. Her recondite nature and finely tuned nervous system have made her a natural sorcerer's apprentice. This

same sensitivity and susceptibility often empowered her to perform little miracles. Countless people have been saved from fires and earthquakes by these intuitive guardians.

"True calendars as pusses eare
Wash't o'er to tell what change is near."
Robert Herrick

Washing may presage a storm, precede sleep, or follow a feast. According to a folk tale, a cat once caught a sparrow who observed, "No gentleman eats before washing his face." The cat relinquished the bird to prove his manners and ~alas~ the finch took flight!

The Cat and the Moon
"The cat went here and there
And the moon spun round like a top
And the nearest kin of the moon,
The creeping cat, looked up.
Black Minnaloushe stared at the moon,
For, wander and wail as he would,
The pure cold light in the sky
Troubled his animal blood....
Minnaloushe creeps through the grass

From moonlit place to place,
The sacred moon overhead
Has taken a new phase.
Does Minnaloushe know that his pupils
Will pass from change to change,
And that from round to crescent,

From crescent to round they range?
Minnaloushe creeps through the grass
Alone, important and wise,
And lifts to the changing moon~
His changing eyes."
W. B. Yeats

"Cats are a mysterious kind of folk. There is more passing in their minds than we are aware⁓."

Sir Walter Scott

The cat has intrigued the monarch and beguiled the mystic. He was waited upon by the priests of Egypt, was companion to Saint Ives and Saint Gertrude, and was sacred to Saint Martha, the friend of Mohammed. The Orientals ascribe to cats "a lan‑ guage, a knowledge of the future, and an extreme sensitiveness which allows them to perceive objects and beings invisible to man." They believe that the feline wavers on the border be‑ tween the conscious and the uncon‑ scious. Baudelaire succinctly captures the enigma of the feline soul⁓

"Peut‑être est‑il fée, est‑il dieu...
Chat mystérieux, chat séraphique,
chat étrange."

Historians, philosophers, and scholars of all disciplines—those whose very livelihood depends on solitary contemplation—have traditionally chosen the cat as their companion. In the long and isolated hours of reverie and reflection they have found solace in the feline's unobtrusive but warming presence. When questions seem overwhelming and answers beyond reach, the soothing serenity found in every cat's eyes helps to ease the frustration of intellectual labours. The cat is learned in the discipline of patience, and his empathetic fellowship is a balm to wearied minds.

"I wish I knew your trick of thought
The perfect balance of your ways:
They seem an inspiration, caught
From other laws in older days."

"The Spectator"

TOWN & COUNTRY REPARTEE

Has any other animal in the course of history been so able to enchant, confound, inspire, and beguile mankind as the cat? From the Cheshire Cat's elusive grin to the noble and triumphant pilgrimage of Dick Whittington's friend, cats have enriched our lives with the delicate nuances of their inimitable personalities. From the silent depths of a cat's mesmerizing gaze, more wisdom is conveyed than is found in the locutions of most men.

He also has the the capacity to vocalize with a complexity of expression that never ceases to amaze us.

"She whysketh with her voyce to
beg and complain,
Another time to testify her
delight and pleasure."
Edward Topsell

One of the enigmatic qualities of the cat is that he is at once unfathomable and infinitely expressive. To communicate with the feline, speak not only

with your voice, but with your eyes and touch as well. Observe your cat. To do so is to learn the language of silence. The feline, noiseless and vivid as a dream, communicates with his eloquent, ever-changing eyes—unblink-ingly intent, dreamingly distracted, or narrowed and inquisitive. Yet they remain filled with that which will always be unknowable. Cat eyes seem a bridge to a world beyond the one we know; so might the eyes of sages appear, or foreseers of the future. Far more tangible is the love reflected there; the gentle gaze, the paw upon your cheek, the affection of one who will remain yours, ever elusive but always loving.

Elizabeth Hamilton once posed the question, "Which is the more beautiful, feline movement or feline stillness?" As

with the most intriguing of queries, the answer eludes us. The movement of cats is the embodiment of grace. Countless dancers and actresses have looked to their cats to try to discover the secret of their fluid rhythms. From the tops of his ears to the tip of his tail, your cat is a richly expressive being. Is his tail

tall and proud, or is it nervously batting the air as he crouches? Are his ears apprehensively flattened back or intently tilted forward to catch sounds we could never hope to hear? In the words of Richard

Austin, "Silence should be alert as cats are, curled before a fire, who note within the flame, the flush of scarlet fen, or eyes as amber as their own."

"We cats are all capable of talking, had we not acquired from human beings a contempt for speech."
Ludwig Tieck

For as long as we have been acquainted with cats, we have been driven to probe and analyze their language—the haunting cries that cut the night, the woeful miaows, the pleasing purr that suggests that all is well in at least one part of the world. Charles Darwin, intrigued by the contented hum of the cat, catalogued seven different purring sounds. The Abbé Galiani distinguished at least twenty variations of the simple mew, while Champfleury patiently taught himself to discern sixty-three different tones! What communicative creatures cats are. They have no speech as we define it, yet

possess the ability to express anger, joy, satisfaction, fear, and affection.

There is, indeed, no single quality of the cat that man could not emulate to his advantage

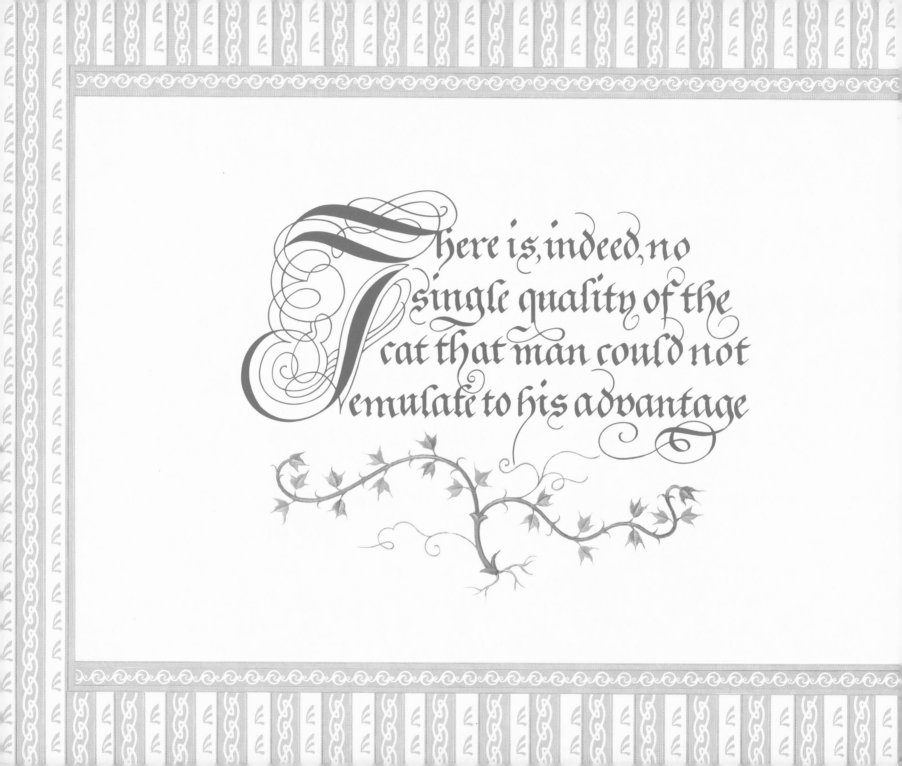

"Half loving-kindliness and
half disdain,
Thou comest to my call serenely suave,
With humming speech and gracious
gestures grave,
In salutation courtly and urbane:
Yet must I humble me thy
grace to gain~
For wiles may win thee, but no
arts enslave,
And nowhere gladly thou
abidest save
Where naught disturbs the concord
of thy reign.

Sphinx of my quiet hearth!
who deignst to dwell
Friend of my toil, companion of
mine ease,

Thine is the lore of Ra and Rameses;
That men forget dost thou
remember well,
Beholden still in blinking reveries,
With sombre sea-green gaze inscrutable."
Graham R. Tomson

"The organization of cats is musical; they are capable of giving many modulations to their voices and in the different passions which occupy them they use different tones."

F.A. Paradis de Moncrif

Few of us would describe feline sounds as lyrical. Their shrill shrieks and plaintive purrs seem far removed from musical cadences. But it seems fair to believe, as did Moncrif, that our problem with the language of cats is not that it is dissonant but rather that it is foreign to our ears. It is as strange, disturbing, and mystifying as Eastern music is to the Westerner or as modern discordant compositions are to the lover of harmonious melodies. Closer in spirit to the feline vocalist are Stravinsky and Sibelius, who, for the first time in Western music, embrace not only the purr but the caterwaul as well.

"It is a difficult matter to gain the affection of a cat. He is a methodical animal tenacious of his own habits, fond of order and neatness, and disinclined to extravagant sentiment. He will be your friend if he deems

you worthy of friendship, but not your slave… Yet what confidence is implicit in his steadfast companionship… He lies for long evenings on your knees, purring contentedly, and forsaking for you the agreeable society of his kind. In vain, melodious mewings on the roof invite him to one of those animated assemblies where fish bones take the place of tea and cake. He is not to be tempted from his post… Sometimes he sits at your feet looking into your face with an expression so gentle and caressing that the depth of his gaze startles you. Who can believe that there is no soul behind those luminous eyes!"

Théophile Gautier

Carl Van Vechten voices his humble and deep-felt admiration for the feline species: "For it is possible, nay probable,

that the cat, unlike man who forgets his previous forms, remembers, really remembers, many generations back; that what we call instinct may be more profound than knowledge. And so Provi-

dence wisely has not allowed the cat to speak any language save his own." But a private language will develop between you and your cat—as intimate and unique as any you share with a dear friend. Who among us never felt the soft brush of a gentle paw upon

a bowed and heavy head? How many cold and lonely midnights have been warmed by the simple presence of this small being, whose affection pervades our solitude?

Town & Country Pleasures

Surely the cat is among the most whimsical of Earth's creatures. Her fancy-free nonchalance and high-spirited joie de vivre have endeared her to all who treasure beauty and imagination. Yet even in her gambols, the cat displays exquisite elegance. To see her leap into the air in quest of a butterfly, ball, or balloon is to witness grace unparalleled. Some cats cling to the hearth; some have wandering souls. There are gregarious cats who enjoy nothing more than a lively party, and shy ones who venture outside familiar terrain only with great timidity. Your cat may be a reclusive philosopher, or she may have the soul of a beachcomber, and love to wander the salty shores with you, searching for crabs, snails, starfish, and all other curiosities the sea has washed upon the sand.

Your cat takes her recreation very seriously. Play is her own civilized

version of what we more commonly refer to as exercise. Not for her those incessant journeys 'round the track or through the field. How much more imaginative is the solitary pursuit of shuffleboard with last night's champagne cork the perfect puck, or a glide across a frozen pond with walnut shells upon her paws—

a favorite pastime of an ingenious Canadian cat. Play is instinctive to your cat, born of her impulse to hunt and the automatic attraction of all carnivores to things that move. If there is no friendly mouse to capture, a kite on a string will

do to keep those muscles supple and that pinpoint coordination on target. To pounce well, your cat must pounce often—.

If you consider music one of life's pleasures, you and your cat can cultivate an appreciation together. Music is a form of expression that perfectly complements your cat's ineffable charm and spirit. She sings vividly and has the most acute of ears, and her fluid motion seems an embodiment of

rhythm's fundamental forms. All cats are responsive to sound and yours

will probably come to take keen pleasure in everything from piano sonatas to rock and roll. She may harmonize in her own distinctive voice, or quietly share in the lull of contentment that is evoked by soft music. As Cicero observed, "Life's pleasures are diminished if not shared with a friend."

Whether wrapping brightly coloured surprises beneath the tree or cutting a cat-sized portion from the Thanksgiving turkey, include your pet in holiday celebrations. Few cats are unmoved by the festivities, so win her heart by letting her share in the fun. She may not be inclined to assist in the wrapping of presents, but she will delight in the shiny crumpled papers and the tantalizing abundance of ribbons and strings just waiting to be tangled. Celebrate her birthday by serving her a hand-made toy mouse sprinkled with a dash of catnip. A brightly coloured toy

Easter egg is sure to tickle her fancy, so hide one in a secret place and watch her pleasure when she discovers it. For Christmas, knit her a cozy covering that she can wear on winter romps, when the chilling wind nips through even the thickest of furs.

Cats winged yearnings journey
Unrestrained
o'er time and space

Some cats love to leap, some are stalkers, and some are sprinters. All cats do all these things in various combinations, but you will find your feline has preferences. She may

be in her element flying after a ball tossed into the air, or scrambling for it in the dark recesses beneath your sofa. The more games and toys you provide, the more fun there will

be for all concerned. You can keep the appeal of old toys fresh by alternating them from week to week so that they will seem new each time she sees them again. In playtime, anything goes, from a scrap of discarded calico to some crumpled tinfoil. A cat at play is charming to watch. Her lustiness and spontaneity express her delight in the world.

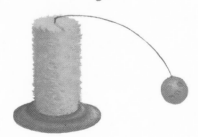

Copine extraordinaire, the cat easily glides into the various roles of companion, playmate, comforter, and even confessor. How many cat lovers can empathize with the affectionate irony of Montaigne's observation, "When I play with my cat, who knows if I amuse myself more with her or she with me?" It is this playful yet supercilious charm that gains our respect as well as our love. Cats find

the world a smorgasbord of savoury pleasures. Introduce your cat to the delights of ribbons and tassels and

feathers. In the ingenious paws of puss your discarded sunbonnet is transformed into headgear, bowl, coverlet, or bed. Learn from each other as you play, and discover the countless pleasures of companionship.

Town & Country Schooling

If independence of spirit, sensitivity, and creativity are the essential components of intelligence, the cat is indeed a gifted creature. There are those who maintain that intelligence in animals is measured solely by obedience, but cat lovers are quick to defend the feline's innate wisdom. Mark Twain once wrote, "Of all God's creatures, there is only one that cannot be made slave to the leash. That one is the cat. If man could be crossed with the cat, it would improve man, but it would deteriorate the cat." Beneath the feline's proud bearing, however, is a nature extremely receptive to the gentle lessons of a loving master. Even the most finicky owner will discover how readily puss can learn to fit in with almost any lifestyle—.

Though capricious at times, the cat is at heart a constant animal. Once his lessons are learned, he will not soon forget them, so it is important to be consistent in your teaching. If you don't want puss on your Queen Anne chair in summertime, you mustn't invite him to snuggle in your lap when the winter nights are snowy and cold. If, in a moment of weak-

ness, he cannot resist clawing that vintage Victorian table leg, a firm and immediate reprimand will inform him of his misdemeanour. Then scoop him up and gently deposit him at his own scratching post so that he will clearly comprehend that this is the proper spot for sharpening his claws. And when he leaps upon the mantelpiece between your crystal candlesticks, do not marvel at his agility. Say no instantly to indicate that this is not well-bred behaviour for a mannerly cat.

Legends, testimonies, and anecdotes abound concerning the feline's acuity. Writer Paula Weiss tells the tale of an entrepreneurial puss who shared

a boutique with its shopkeepers, whose living quarters were upstairs. If they were at lunch or at rest, the young cat would mind the store. Settling himself comfortably by the till, he would alert the storeowners to the arrival of prospective customers by tugging on a bell pull. A more heroic tale involves a feline who lived with his mistress and her canary. During the Second World War, when London was being bombed, these three would take cover beneath the dining room table when there was no time to reach the shelter. One day while the lady was collecting her wash on the front porch, tabby suddenly dashed inside and hid under the table. His mistress took heed and quickly followed, cage in hand-minutes before the entire porch was destroyed by an explosion.

Your town cat will love to accompany you on your perambulations down the busy avenues. With a little patience, you can easily teach him to stroll by your side on a leash taking

in all the sights and sounds of the city. If your puss is timorous, you may want to restrict your jaunts to quiet sidewalks. Bolder felines warm to the bustle of crowded streets, tirelessly exploring the colorful byways. Though cats can be taught to wear either collar or harness, the latter is preferable since it puts less strain on your pet's delicate neck. Introduce him to his new harness as if it is a toy, perhaps sprinkling it with catnip to engage his interest. After a few days of initiation, slip it gently on while applauding his

cooperation. Once he has become used to indoor strolls, embark upon your urban voyage———.

In a
Cats Eye
all things belong
to Cats

Establishing a rapport between you and your cat is a necessary element in training your feline to acquiesce to your desires. While other pets may prefer nothing more than a simple yes or no to express our delight or displeasure, the cat is generally a creature of nuance. Talk to him as much as possible. With remarkable alacrity, he will learn to respond to various intonations of your voice and to relate these tones to the different demands they impart. This is not to say that a firm and simple no does not play an important role in your relationship. With repetition, your feline will soon come to realize that there are some things in your world that he cannot share. Define the boundaries you wish to

construct. The bond between you and your cat is a subtle thing—a fabric woven by threads of trust, tenderness, habit, and the mutual desire to understand each other's needs.

We speak of the cat as being alternately charming and imperious, affectionate and aloof. Despite his mercurial temperament, there are ways of convincing your feline to consistently respond to your requests. Essentially, you do not so much teach your cat as bribe him. The challenge is to communicate to your cat that what you are asking him to do is not merely in your best interests, but in his own as well. Tempt him with treats. If a sample of salmon or a demitasse of milk awaits him when you call,

your cat will quickly make an appearance. If, on the other hand, you wish him to refrain from prancing about in the begonias

and geraniums, a dash of hot pepper sprinkled on the soil will quickly convince him to find greener playgrounds. Grow a catnip plant he can call his own, and learn to be a master in the fine art of persuasion.

Town & Country Kitchen

While enjoying the welcoming purr and gently gleaming eyes of your cat, remember that her well-being depends on a balanced diet. It is not necessary to serve a gourmet delight; however, if you choose to spice up your feline's life with the zesty flavours of international cuisines, be sure to keep sound nutrition in mind. Wheat germ and brewer's yeast are healthful condiments, and cod liver oil adds lustre and body to her coat. Provide a wholesome treat to help your cat digest a pill or reward desirable behaviour. A cantaloupe ball or pitted olive is especially fun to pounce upon or nibble on. A high quality diet will have a positive effect on her temperament, and the fur of a healthy feline exudes a lovely perfume—.

"When Human Folk at Table eat
A kitten must not mew for meat,
Or jump to grab it from the Dish,
(Unless it happens to be fish)."
Oliver Herford

That I want a modest share
Of the good things that are there.
If he pay but scanty heed
To my little stomach's need,

"Always well behaved am I,
Never scratch and never cry;
Only touch the diner's hand,
So that he can understand

I beg him with a mew polite
To give me just a single bite.
Greedy though the diner be,
He will share his meal with me."
Madame Deshoullières

Asparagus Tip Parmesan

To celebrate the San Gennaro festival, spice one tender green asparagus tip with a splash of your favourite marinara sauce and a sprinkle of freshly grated Romano and Parmesan cheese—.

Pâté Maison

Cook one half pound of liver until firm. Put it into your meat grinder and—voilà!—chopped liver. A tablespoon of soybean oil will settle your cat's tummy; supplemental vitamins add nourishment. Add a soupçon of salt. Serve sans garnish or mix with a canned food.

Guacamole

Mash well one slice of ripened avocado. Add a teaspoon of finely chopped alfalfa sprouts high in nutrients for your pet. A dash of bran instead of taco chips and your cat will have a Mexican fiesta.

Fruits de Mer

While preparing Coquilles St. Jacques or some other seafood delight for your family, set aside bits of lobster, crab, shrimp, oyster, clams, or mussels for your puss. Forego the béchamel sauce, since felines prefer their fish plain.

Bifteck Tartare

Strictly for epicurean tastes. Cut one half pound of beef into bite-size pieces. Beat an egg until yolk and white are blended, then mix well into the meat. Add a soupçon of garlic salt.

Herbal Tea

Spice a saucer of English tea with a fresh mint leaf from your garden and a dappling of honey.

the
world is so full
of a number of mice
I'm sure that we all
should be happy
and nice

In many dwellings, the kitchen hearth is Kitty's domain. As you prepare your favourite recipe, your cat will attentively follow your every movement, unless her attention is captured by an errant mouse. As Chaucer whimsically noted in the Manciple's Tale ———:

"Take a cat, nourish it well with milk
And tender meat, make it a couch of silk,
But let it see a mouse along the wall
And it abandons milk and meat and all,
Aye, every other dainty in the house,
Such is its appetite to eat a mouse.
You see, a natural lust is in possession
And appetite has banished its discretion."

Robert Herrick's pastoral puss boasts of his country comforts to his town-bred brother:

"Yet can thy humble roof maintaine
a quire
Of singing crickets by the fire;
And the brisk mouse may feast
herselfe with crumbs,
Till that green-eyed kilting comes."

"As for the astounding instances of feline generosity which we are daily requested to consider, they would lead us to suppose that cats live only to do good. Gautier's little Bohemian, who

shared his dinner occasionally with disreputable friends out of pure love for low company, shines but dimly by comparison with the small Saint Elizabeths, who apparently have no use for their dinners save to give them to all the poor and starving cats in the neighbourhood.... Mr. Larrabee is responsible for the edifying history of a Norman cat whose conscience was troubled by the overabundance of her supplies. Accordingly, she brought home one day a lean cottage animal to share the feast; observing which, her master laid out for her a double portion the next morning. This continued until she had twenty pensioners around her generous board."

Agnes Repplier

Town & Country Squire

The twilight years of your feline's life will be a time of deep and peaceful happiness, enhanced by the accumulated wisdom of experience and enriched by time. Many cat owners find their relationship with their pet deepening, incorporating a mutual trust and affection at once enduring and bittersweet. Love and dependence become more inextricably entwined than at any other moment in your cat's life. Although he may have always spent most of his day snoozing, his need for sleep will now intensify. He will awaken and blink drowsily as he returns your affectionate gaze, then sink back into the nether land of dreams he so delights in. The older cat seems filled with serenity as his sleeping and waking worlds become a somnolent whole.

As you care for your older cat, be especially responsive to his growing needs. More than ever, he will appreciate consistency and routine. Celebrate the simple rituals of food, rest, and recreation, and particularly cherish those times reserved for fondling. It is essential to play with your cat as he ages. For now, although he has less desire to frolic and sport, he needs exercise

more than ever to keep him lithe and full of vitality. Set aside as many moments as you can to amuse him with his favourite toys. That

worn patchwork mouse still holds fascination as it peers with button eyes from the tempting hideout you have chosen. So does the ball of brightly coloured yarn unravelled across the porch. The frisky kitten will emerge as you romp together.

Although the squire may be subdued, do not assume that he is being reclusive. He will retain his grace and beauty to an advanced age, but his legs will not serve him as they once did. He may not be able to leap as lightly upon your lap or dart to the

foyer to welcome you home. As he sits contemplatively sequestered amid his dreams, speak to him softly to reassure him of your presence. Approach him often. Do not be afraid to shower him with tenderness. The aging cat will crave any form of tactile communication, since his other means of perception are not as sharp as they once were. Your loving touch will help him remain responsive to his surroundings. Indulge him with a daily grooming session. Not only will he bask in the attention, he will appreciate the help, since the flexibility that allowed him to spruce himself from tail to toe has been diminished with age.

"He shared the life of the household, with that enjoyment of quiet fireside friendship which is a characteristic of

cats. He had his own place on the hearth, and would sit there for hours, listening to conversation with a well-bred air of intelligence and interest. He glanced occasionally from speaker to speaker, and addressed them with little half-articulate sounds, as though protesting politely against their state-ments, or offering an opinion of his own upon the matter under dis-cussion. He loved books, and, when he found one open upon the table, would lie down on it, turn over the edges of the leaves with his paw, and, after a time, fall asleep, for all the world as if he had been reading a fashionable novel."

Théophile Gautier

The Retired Cat
" I know not where she
caught the trick,~
Nature perhaps herself had cast her
In such a mould 'philosophique,'
Or else she learned it
of her Master,
Sometimes ascending, 'debonnaire,'
An apple-tree, or lofty pear,

Lodged with convenience in the fork,
She watched the gardener
at his work;
Sometimes her ease and solace sought
In an old empty watering-pot;
There wanting nothing save a fan,
To seem some nymph in her sedan,
Apparelled in exactest sort,
And ready to be borne to Court"
William Cowper

" You are life's true philosopher to
whom all moralists are one~."

Anonymous

I love Cats because
I love my Home
And after a while they become
Its visible Soul

As the end of his life approaches and his sense of territory narrows with his curtailed wanderings, your cat will more and more appreciate those familiar daily rituals that re-assure him when he feels his own

power lessening. And as his self~re-liance decreases, he needs you to com-fort him. In his youth he may have made it clear that you were nice but hardly necessary; now you are

an essential part of his world. He must learn to be dependent without losing his dignity. But he is more able now to show just how much he does care, removed from the restraints that the drive for independence can put on love's expression.

TOWN & COUNTRY TALES

While curled before the winter fire, listening to hush of snow upon the windowpane, it is nice to ponder feline lore and legends. Among these fables is the Polish tale of the Pussy Willow⁓.

"A lot of little kittens were thrown into a river to drown. On the banks the mother cat wept so loud and long that the willows in sympathy consulted together as to what to do. They held out their long branches like mooring lines, and the little kittens, in desperation, clung to them. Ever since then, every spring, the willow-without-a-flower decks itself out in those gentle velvet buds that feel to the fingers like the silky coat of a small cat. In every land these soft willow trees are named after cats."

"Mary, the daughter of Charles Dickens nostalgically writes in "My Father as I Recall Him"———:

"One evening we were all, except father, going to a ball, and when we started, we left 'the master' and his cat in the drawing-room together. 'The Master' was reading at a small table; suddenly

the candle went out. My father, who was much interested in his book,

relighted the candle, stroked the cat, who was looking at him pathetically he noticed, and continued his reading.

A few minutes later, as the light became dim, he looked up just in time to see puss deliberately put out the candle with his paw, and then look appealingly at him. This second and unmistakable hint was not disregarded and puss was given the petting he craved.""

"There was once a very beautiful cat called Gon, with fur as smooth and shining as silk and the most beautiful green eyes, who belonged to a music teacher...Not far away there lived a most beautiful little cat, with soft fur and a nose like marzipan and large, loving eyes. She was called Koma...One night they met, and fell at once deeply

in love....They wanted to spend their whole lives together (but) their owners

were so afraid of losing them that they kept them almost as prisoners...

and they at length sadly decided that they must leave their kind master and mistress and go out into the wide world.....one dark night they both slipped away.....They went on, day after day...until they came to the great...Imperial Palace.....They felt that this was a place to live, and they were licking eachother tenderly under a flowering tree when...

a great mastiff rushed up to attack them. Koma shot up the tree, but Gon turned to defend her.... One of the Palace attendants ran up with a stick and drove the dog away. He saw what a beautiful cat Gon was

and took him... to present him to the Princess.... The Princess was delighted with Gon...and could hardly bear him out of her sight; but where was Koma?... One day, as he was

lying by the window looking out he saw a great hulking Tom Cat bullying...a little Tib. Full of rage he...went to the rescue. Then he turned to comfort the little lady cat and...saw that it was his own Koma..... Gon led his little wife proudly to the Palace and together they told the Princess all their story. She wept with pity for them, and promised that they should never be separated again——."

A cat maie looke
on a king ye know

In India the cunning Patripatan, "once climbed into the land of Devendiren in the sky~where, as we all know, there reigned twenty-four million gods and forty-eight million goddesses. In order to plead his master's cause, he became the friend of the all-powerful king of the gods and the beloved confidant

of the most beautiful of the god-desses. He did so much and so well that for three hundred years he forgot

to come down again to the earth. And while the prince and the

inhabitants of the kingdom of Salangham awaited his return, not a person aged by a single hour during all the hours and days and years that passed. At last Patripatan returned. In his white paws he brought a complete and heavy branch of that rarest talis-man~flower of Parasidam, in full flower. And from that day there was nothing but gentleness and beauty in that kingdom."

"'Prince,' said the White Cat, 'let us be merry. I have ordered a naval combat between my cats and the terrible rats of this country.'... The ships in which the cats embarked were made of pieces of cork, and sailed buoyantly over the waves. The rats had joined together a number of egg-shells, and into these their sailors bravely climbed. The battle was hard fought.... Minagrobis, admiral of the feline fleet... attacked and promptly devoured the enemy's great captain, a wise and experienced old rat... whose death filled his followers with despair. The White Cat would not, however, permit the

destruction of the enemy. She was a sagacious ruler, and she knew that if there were no more rats and mice left in the land, her subjects would live in idleness, which is a dangerous thing, and might make them disobedient and rebellious."

Marie De Berneville

I gratefully acknowledge the permission to quote from the books cited herein, although many other sources provided hours of delightful reading and inspiration.

Artiste~From "The Tiger in the House" by Carl Van Vechten. Copyright©1920, 1936 by Carl Van Vechten. Reprinted by permission of Alfred A. Knopf, Inc. p. 276. Charles Baudelaire from "Cats: A Celebration" 1979, Elizabeth Hamilton. Reprinted with the permission of Charles Scribner's Sons. In Great Britain, reprinted with the permission of David & Charles, Brunel House, Newton Abbot, p. 46. Algernon Charles Swinburne, from Agnes Repplier, "The Fireside Sphinx," Boston and New York: Houghton Mifflin and Co., 1901, p. 282. Louis MacNeice from "Cats: A Celebration", p. 54. Neville Braybrooke: Reprinted by permission of "The Tablet" 48 Great Peter's Street, London. Champfleury (pseudonym of Jules Husson) from "The Tiger in the House," p. 212. Courtship~Mark Van Doren: Reprinted by permission of Hill and Wang, a division of Farrar, Straus, & Giroux, Inc. From "The Midwife" from "Collected and New Poems 1924-1963" by Mark Van Doren Copyright©1963 by Mark Van Doren. J.W. Hackett from "Haiku Poetry," Vol. III p. 25. Reprinted from the edition published by Japan Publications, Inc. Pierre Jean de Béranger from "The Tiger in the House," p. 265. George Huddesford: Ibid, p. 274. Madame Deshoullières: Ibid, p. 264. Théophile Gautier from "The Fireside Sphinx," p. 210. Hiddigeigei: Joseph Victor von Scheffel's "Der Trompeter von Säkkingem," from "The Tiger in the House," p. 194. Aesop's Fable from Repplier, "The Cat," New York: Sturgis and Walton Company, 1912. p. 131. Repplier, "The Fireside Sphinx," p. 183. Temperament~Repplier, "The Fireside Sphinx." St. George Mivart, from "The Tiger in the House," p. 48. Van Vechten, op. cit. p. 47. Fernand Méry, from "Le Chat, Son Histoire, Sa Vie, et Sa Magique." Reprinted by permission of Les Editions Robert Laffonte: Paris and Madison Square Press, Grosset and Dunlap, Inc. New York, 1968. In Great Britain by permission of Paul Hamlyn Ltd. Jules Lemaître, from "The Cat." Van Vechten, op. cit. p. 48. François René de

Châteaubriand: Ibid, p.3. Spectator, The, from "The Cat," p.32. Méry, from "The Tiger in the House." Kitten~Champfleury from "The Cat," p.20. F.A. Paradis de Moncrif from "The Fireside Sphinx." Oliver Herford from "The Tiger in the House," p.260. Mivart: Ibid, p.5. Repplier, "The Fireside Sphinx." Hamilton, op. cit. p.52. Philip Gilbert Hamerton from "The Cat." William Wordsworth, from "The Fireside Sphinx." Repplier: Ibid, p.260. Care~Hippolyte Taine from "The Cat," p.33. Scholar~ Oliver Goldsmith from "The Fireside Sphinx," p.138. Repplier: Ibid, p.6. Robert Herrick: Ibid, p.131. William Butler Yeats, "The Cat and the Moon." Used with permission of Macmillan Publishing Co., Inc. from "The Collected Poems of W.B. Yeats" Copyright ©1919 by Macmillan Publishing Co., Inc., renewed 1947 by Bertha Georgie Yeats. Used in Great Britain by permission of Michael and Anne Yeats and Macmillan London, Ltd. Sir Walter Scott from "The Tiger in the House," p.82. Van Vechten, op. cit. p.93. Baudelaire: Ibid, p.81. Spectator, The, from "The Fireside Sphinx," p.290. Repartee~Edward Topsell from "Cats: A Celebration," p.115. Hamilton, op. cit. p.120. Richard Austin: Ibid, p.118. Ludwig Tieck: Ibid, p.114. Graham R. Tomson from "The

Fireside Sphinx," p.281. Moncrif from "The Tiger in the House," p.191. Théophile Gautier from "The Fireside Sphinx," p.209. Van Vechten, op. cit. p.304. Schooling~ Stories from "Cats: A Celebration." Kitchen~Deshoullieres from "The Cat." Geoffrey Chaucer: Reprinted from "The Canterbury Tales" Translated by Nevill Coghill, Penguin Classics, revised edition 1977. Copyright 1951 by Nevill Coghill. Copyright 1958, 1960, 1975, 1977. Reprinted by permission of Penguin Books Ltd. Herrick from "The Tiger in the House," p.249. Repplier, "The Fireside Sphinx." Squire~ Gautier from "The Fireside Sphinx," p.207. William Cowper from "The Cat." Anonymous from "The Fireside Sphinx," p.289. Tales~Pussy Willow Tale: from Méry, "Le Chat, Son Histoire, Sa Vie, et Sa Magique," p.49. Gon~Reprinted by permission of the estate of the late Katherine M. Briggs. Taken from "Nine Lines" by Katherine M. Briggs. Courtesy of Routledge and Kegan Paul Ltd. London. Patripatan: op. cit. p.49. The Sea Battle: Marie de Berneville (Comtesse d'Aulnoy), "La Chatte Blanche" from "The Cat," p.167.

Proverbs: January~ Leonardo Da Vinci. February~
French saying. March~ Jules Lemaître. April~ Graham Tomson. May~ "The Nation".
June~ Erasmus Darwin. July~ Carl Van Vechten. August~ Hiddigeigei. September~ English
saying. October~ Oliver Herford. November~ Jean Cocteau. December~ John Heywood.